SWEATERS
OPTIONS

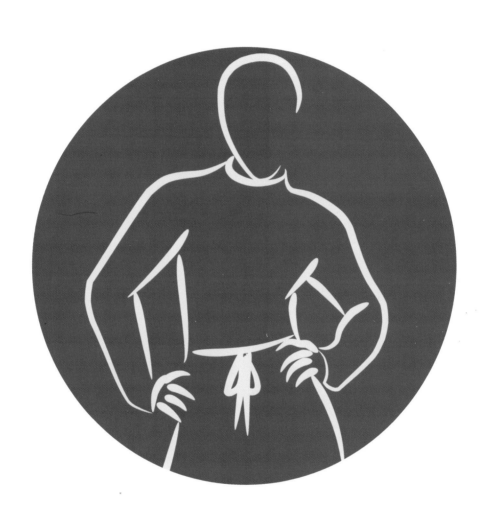

LEISURE ARTS, INC.
Little Rock, Arkansas

SWEATERS
OPTIONS

Want to *love* every sweater you knit?

With this collection from Leisure Arts, you'll make sweaters you adore from start to finish! That's because we're helping you **choose** the yarn brand and color you prefer. And you'll know — before you begin knitting — how your finished sweater will look!

All of Leisure Arts' exciting new **Options** books show you not only the original designer creation, but also a second version in an entirely different yarn. The delightful results in *Options: Sweaters* are a collection of five **stylish** garments in **two** yarn variations by popular knitwear designer Deborah Newton.

It's time to create the sweater that's truly perfect for you!

EDITORIAL STAFF

Vice President and Editor-in-Chief: Sandra Graham Case. *Executive Director of Publications:* Cheryl Nodine Gunnells. *Senior Director of Publications:* Susan White Sullivan. *Director of Designer Relations:* Debra Nettles. *Director of Retail Marketing:* Stephen Wilson. *Art Operations Director:* Jeff Curtis. *Special Projects Coordinator:* Mary Sullivan Hutcheson. TECHNICAL — *Technical Writer:* Linda Luder. *Editorial Writer:* Susan McManus Johnson. ART — *Art Publications Director:* Rhonda Hodge Shelby. *Art Imaging Director:* Mark Hawkins. *Senior Publications Designer:* Dana Vaughn. *Imaging Technician:* Mark R. Potter. *Photography Stylist:* Cassie Francioni. *Contributing Photographer:* Jason Masters. *Publishing Systems Administrator:* Becky Riddle. *Publishing Systems Assistants:* Clint Hanson, Josh Hyatt, and John Rose.

BUSINESS STAFF

Chief Operating Officer: Tom Siebenmorgen. *Vice President, Sales and Marketing:* Pam Stebbins. *Director of Sales and Services:* Margaret Reinold. *Vice President, Operations:* Jim Dittrich. *Comptroller, Operations:* Rob Thieme. *Retail Customer Service Manager:* Stan Raynor. *Print Production Manager:* Fred F. Pruss.

ISBN 1-57486-585-4

10 9 8 7 6 5 4 3 2 1

MEET Deborah Newton

Deborah Newton's journey into creativity started early in her life, and it has yielded a few surprising moments.

Perhaps the most memorable occurred the first time she sold a design to a nationally known needlework magazine. Deborah eagerly awaited the appearance of her sweater on the periodical's glossy pages.

"When the magazine was printed," says Deborah, "I opened up my copy, and there was my sweater — turned the wrong way on the model! They had no idea it was being worn backwards."

Since those early days, Deborah's designs have been published in numerous magazines without further mishaps. And Deborah's book, *Designing Knitwear*, is considered a classic in design circles.

When Deborah isn't developing new patterns, she's busy assisting her brother with his map-making business. Deborah helps by writing, researching, marketing, and shipping the educational maps to schools in all fifty states. Deborah finds the work very rewarding.

"We're helping to educate children about the world," she says. "We have a program that supplies a 'Geography Question of the Day.' And there are unfinished maps that allow kids to draw in the details."

Deborah also works in her community garden and has been active in yoga for the past ten years. "I thoroughly enjoy yoga. I even travel to Boston to learn from a world-famous teacher."

And Deborah finds life at home is never dull. "My life partner is Paul Di Filippo, the science fiction writer. We've been together for several years. His creativity still amazes me."

With such a full life, we wondered how Deborah ever had time to get involved in designing knit items.

"I've knitted all my life, so it was a natural transition. I learned to knit from my mother before I was old enough to start school. I loved it. It clicked immediately with me. I knitted all through my school years and ended up with an English degree and still had a desire to design my own knitwear. My freelance designing really started in 1982. I've also been a contributing writer for knitting magazines.

"When your hobby becomes your work, you learn that life offers a lot of surprises that can be very pleasant."

CONTENTS

Short & Saucy 26

Divine Asymmetry 36

WARM THOUGHTS **OPTION** ①

Whether you knit this medium-weight sweater for yourself or for someone else, the **drawstring** waist will help you achieve a custom fit. And the café-au-lait color of this cabled design is a toasty **treat** for the eyes.

If the **warm** hue of coffee doesn't stir your soul, perhaps you have a **passion** for purple? The same sweater in a royal hue lives in the realm of cool colors, while the soft yarn retains all the **coziness** you want.

OPTION 2

Option 1

Classic Elite Yarns, Inc. Lush
Medium/Worsted Weight Yarn
  [1³/₄ ounces, 124 yards
  (50 grams, 113 meters) per skein]:
  #4438 Latte - 12{14-16} skeins
Straight knitting needles, size 7 (4.5 mm) **or** size
  needed for gauge
16" (40.5 cm) Circular knitting needle,
  size 7 (4.5 mm)
Crochet hook, size H (5 mm)
Cable needle
Stitch holders - 2
Yarn needle

GAUGE: In Stockinette Stitch,
  20 sts and 28 rows = 4" (10 cm)
  In Cable & Rib pattern,
  24 sts and 28 rows = 4" (10 cm)

WARM THOUGHTS ◼◼◼▭ INTERMEDIATE

Option 2

Bernat® Satin
Medium/Worsted Weight Yarn
  [3¹/₂ ounces, 163 yards
  (100 grams, 149 meters) per skein]:
  #04307 Sultana - 9{10-11} skeins
Straight knitting needles, size 7 (4.5 mm) **or** size
  needed for gauge
16" (40.5 cm) Circular knitting needle,
  size 7 (4.5 mm)
Crochet hook, size H (5 mm)
Cable needle
Stitch holders - 2
Yarn needle

GAUGE: In Stockinette Stitch,
  20 sts and 28 rows = 4" (10 cm)
  In Cable & Rib pattern,
  24 sts and 28 rows = 4" (10 cm)

Size	Finished Chest Measurement
Small	38½" (98 cm)
Medium	43¼" (110 cm)
Large	48" (122 cm)

Size Note: Instructions are written for size Small with sizes Medium and Large in braces { }. Instructions will be easier to read if you circle all the numbers pertaining to your size. If only one number is given, it applies to all sizes.

STITCH GUIDE
CABLE (uses 4 sts)
Slip next 2 sts onto cable needle and hold in **back** of work, K2 from left needle, K2 from cable needle.

BACK
Cast on 118{132-146} sts.

Row 1 (Right side): K2, P2, ★ (K2, P2) twice, K4, P2; repeat from ★ across to last 2 sts, K2.

Row 2: P2, K2, ★ P4, K2, (P2, K2) twice; repeat from ★ across to last 2 sts, P2.

Row 3: K2, P2, ★ (K2, P2) twice, work Cable, P2; repeat from ★ across to last 2 sts, K2.

Row 4: P2, K2, ★ P4, K2, (P2, K2) twice; repeat from ★ across to last 2 sts, P2.

Row 5: K2, P2, ★ (K2, P2) twice, K4, P2; repeat from ★ across to last 2 sts, K2.

Row 6: P2, K2, ★ P4, K2, (P2, K2) twice; repeat from ★ across to last 2 sts, P2.

Row 7: K2, P2, ★ [K2, K2 tog (*Fig. 1, page 46*), YO (*Fig. 6a, page 47*)] twice, K4, P2; repeat from ★ across to last 2 sts, K2.

Row 8: P2, K2, (P 12, K2) across to last 2 sts, P2.

Row 9: K2, P2, ★ K1, K2 tog, YO, K2, K2 tog, YO, K1, work Cable, P2; repeat from ★ across to last 2 sts, K2.

Row 10: P2, K2, (P 12, K2) across to last 2 sts, P2.

Row 11: K2, P2, ★ K2 tog, YO, K2, K2 tog, YO, K6, P2; repeat from ★ across to last 2 sts, K2.

Row 12: P2, K2, (P 12, K2) across to last 2 sts, P2.

Row 13: K2, P2, ★ K1, YO, SSK (*Figs. 3a-c, page 46*), K2, YO, SSK, K5, P2; repeat from ★ across to last 2 sts, K2.

Row 14: P2, K2, (P 12, K2) across to last 2 sts, P2.

Row 15: K2, P2, ★ (K2, YO, SSK) twice, work Cable, P2; repeat from ★ across to last 2 sts, K2.

Row 16: P2, K2, (P 12, K2) across to last 2 sts, P2.

Row 17: K2, P2, ★ K3, YO, SSK, K2, YO, SSK, K3, P2; repeat from ★ across to last 2 sts, K2.

Row 18: P2, K2, ★ P4, K2, (P2, K2) twice; repeat from ★ across to last 2 sts, P2.

Row 19: K2, P2, ★ (K2, P2) twice, K4, P2; repeat from ★ across to last 2 sts, K2.

Row 20: P2, K2, ★ P4, K2, (P2, K2) twice; repeat from ★ across to last 2 sts, P2.

Row 21: K2, P2, ★ (K2, P2) twice, work Cable, P2; repeat from ★ across to last 2 sts, K2.

Row 22: P2, K2, ★ P4, K2, (P2, K2) twice; repeat from ★ across to last 2 sts, P2.

Row 23: K2, P2, ★ (K2, P2) twice, K4, P2; repeat from ★ across to last 2 sts, K2.

Row 24: P2, K2, ★ P4, K2, (P2, K2) twice; repeat from ★ across to last 2 sts, P2.

Repeat Rows 1-24 until piece measures approximately 18" (45.5 cm) from cast on edge, ending by working a **wrong** side row.

Instructions continued on page 10.

ARMHOLE SHAPING

Maintain established pattern throughout and maintain 2 edge sts worked in Stockinette Stitch at **each** Armhole edge.

Rows 1 and 2: Bind off 6{7-8} sts, work across in pattern: 106{118-130} sts.

Rows 3 thru 4{6-6}: Bind off 2{2-3} sts, work across in pattern: 102{110-118} sts.

Decrease Row: K1, SSK, work across in pattern to last 3 sts, K2 tog, K1: 100{108-116} sts.

Next Row: Work across in pattern.

Repeat last 2 rows, 3{4-5} times; then repeat Decrease Row once **more**: 92{98-104} sts.

Work even until Armholes measure approximately 8{8¹/₂-9}"/20.5{21.5-23} cm, ending by working a **right** side row.

NECK AND SHOULDER SHAPING

Both sides of Neck are worked at the same time, using separate yarn for **each** side. Maintain established pattern throughout.

Row 1: Bind off 8{8-9} sts at Armhole edge, work across in pattern until there are 27{28-29} sts on the right needle, slip next 22{26-28} sts onto st holder; with second yarn, bind off 5 sts at Neck edge, work in pattern across remaining sts.

Row 2: Bind off 8{8-9} sts at Armhole edge, work across in pattern; with second yarn, bind off 5 sts at Neck edge, work across in pattern: 22{23-24} sts **each** side.

Rows 3 and 4: Bind off 8{9-9} sts at Armhole edge, work across in pattern; with second yarn, bind off 5 sts at Neck edge, work across in pattern: 9{9-10} sts **each** side.

Row 5: Bind off all sts on first side; with second yarn, work across in pattern.

Bind off remaining sts.

FRONT

Work same as Back until Armholes measure approximately 6{6¹/₂-7}"/15{16.5-18} cm, ending by working a **right** side row: 92{98-104} sts.

NECK SHAPING

Both sides of Neck are worked at the same time, using separate yarn for **each** side. Maintain established pattern throughout.

Row 1: Work in pattern across 35{36-38} sts, slip next 22{26-28} sts onto st holder, making note of last row of Cable pattern worked; with second yarn, work in pattern across remaining sts: 35{36-38} sts **each** side.

Rows 2-5: Work across in pattern; with second yarn, bind off 5 sts at Neck edge, work across in pattern: 25{26-28} sts **each** side.

Work even until Front measures same as Back to Shoulder Shaping, ending by working a **right** side row.

SHOULDER SHAPING

Rows 1 and 2: Bind off 8{8-9} sts at Armhole edge, work across in pattern; with second yarn, work across in pattern: 17{18-19} sts **each** side.

Rows 3 and 4: Bind off 8{9-9} sts at Armhole edge, work across in pattern; with second yarn, work across in pattern: 9{9-10} sts **each** side.

Row 5: Bind off all sts on first side; with second yarn, work across in pattern.

Bind off remaining sts.

SLEEVE (Make 2)

Cast on 48 sts.

Row 1 (Right side)**:** K2, P2, ★ (K2, P2) twice, K4, P2; repeat from ★ across to last 2 sts, K2.

Row 2: P2, K2, ★ P4, K2, (P2, K2) twice; repeat from ★ across to last 2 sts, P2.

Row 3: K2, P2, ★ (K2, P2) twice, work Cable, P2; repeat from ★ across to last 2 sts, K2.

Row 4: P2, K2, ★ P4, K2, (P2, K2) twice; repeat from ★ across to last 2 sts, P2.

Row 5: K2, P2, ★ (K2, P2) twice, K4, P2; repeat from ★ across to last 2 sts, K2.

Row 6: P2, K2, ★ P4, K2, (P2, K2) twice; repeat from ★ across to last 2 sts, P2.

Row 7 (Increase row): K2, M1 (*Figs. 4a & b, page 46*), P2, ★ (K2, K2 tog, YO) twice, K4, P2; repeat from ★ across to last 2 sts, M1, K2: 50 sts.

Continuing in pattern same as Back and maintaining 2 edge sts worked in Stockinette Stitch at each edge, increase one st at **each** edge in same manner, every 4th row, 0{3-12} times (*see Zeros, page 44*); then increase every 6th row, 11{16-10} times; then every 8th row, 5{0-0} times: 82{88-94} sts.

Work even until Sleeve measures approximately 17½{18-18}"/44.5{45.5-45.5} cm from cast on edge, ending by working a **wrong** side row.

SLEEVE CAP

Rows 1 and 2: Bind off 6{7-8} sts, work across in pattern: 70{74-78} sts.

Rows 3 and 4: Bind off 2{2-3} sts, work across in pattern: 66{70-72} sts.

Row 5 (Decrease row): K1, SSK, work across in pattern to last 3 sts, K2 tog, K1: 64{68-70} sts.

Row 6: Work across in pattern.

Rows 7 thru 38{42-44}: Repeat Rows 5 and 6, 16{18-19} times: 32 sts.

Next 4 Rows: Bind off 2 sts, work across in pattern: 24 sts.

Bind off remaining sts.

FINISHING

Sew shoulder seams.

Sew Sleeves into armholes matching bound off sts at underarm and placing center of Cap at shoulder seam.

Weave underarm and side in one continuous seam (*Fig. 9, page 48*).

NECK RIBBING

With **right** side facing, using circular needle and beginning at right shoulder seam, pick up 12 sts along Right Back Neck edge (*Figs. 8a & b, page 48*), work in pattern across sts on Back st holder, pick up 12 sts along Left Back Neck edge, pick up 20{21-19} sts along Left Front Neck edge, work in pattern across sts on Front st holder, pick up 20{19-21} sts along Right Front Neck edge; place marker to mark beginning of rnd (*see Markers, page 44*): 108{116-120} sts.

Rnd 1: (K2, P2) 18{18-20} times, work next row of Cable across next 4 sts, P2, (K2, P2) twice, work next row of Cable across next 4 sts, P2, (K2, P2) around.

Repeat Rnd 1 until ribbing measures approximately 2½" (6.5 cm).

Bind off all sts in pattern.

CORD

With crochet hook, make a chain approximately 45" (114.5 cm) to 50" (127 cm) long (*Fig. 11, page 49*).

Slip st in second ch from hook (*Fig. 12, page 49*) and in each ch across; finish off (*see Finishing Off, page 49*).

Try on Pullover and weave Cord through an eyelet row at desired point below bust, beginning at center front.

Make 2 pom-poms (*Figs. 10a-c, page 49*) and attach one to each end of Cord.

OPTION 1

Blue diamonds have always been highly prized. And this blue sweater with a **diamond eyelet** pattern will certainly be a **valued** part of your wardrobe. Pair it with your favorite skirt or slacks for an outfit you'll **treasure**.

This **jewel** of a V-neck design can't be found in stores. But you can create it in any color you can **imagine**. This second option is fashioned of bulky-weight yarn in brown tones with a **golden gleam**.

OPTION 2

Option 1

Classic Elite Yarns Beatrice
Bulky Weight Yarn
  [1³/₄ ounces, 63 yards
  (50 grams, 58 meters) per skein]:
  #3292 Bea's Blue - 13{15-17} skeins
Straight knitting needles, size 10 (6 mm) **or** size
  needed for gauge
Markers
Yarn needle

GAUGE: In Reverse Stockinette Stitch,
      14 sts and 20 rows = 4" (10 cm)
      In pattern, 21 sts = 6" (15.25 cm)

GIRL'S BEST FRIEND  INTERMEDIATE

Option 2

Lion Brand® Moonlight Mohair
Bulky Weight Yarn
  [1³/₄ ounces, 82 yards
  (50 grams, 75 meters) per skein]:
  #203 Safari - 10{11-12} skeins
Straight knitting needles, size 10 (6 mm) **or** size
  needed for gauge
Markers
Yarn needle

GAUGE: In Reverse Stockinette Stitch,
      14 sts and 20 rows = 4" (10 cm)
      In pattern, 21 sts = 6" (15.25 cm)

Size	Finished Chest Measurement
Small	40½" (103 cm)
Medium	44" (112 cm)
Large	48½" (123 cm)

Size Note: Instructions are written for size Small with sizes Medium and Large in braces { }. Instructions will be easier to read if you circle all the numbers pertaining to your size. If only one number is given, it applies to all sizes.

BACK

Cast on 73{79-87} sts.

Row 1: Knit across.

Row 2: Purl across.

Row 3 (Right side): K2, P 14{17-21}, place marker (*see Markers, page 44*), K1 tbl (*Fig. A, page 45*), ★ P6, P2 tog (*Fig. 2, page 46*), YO (*Fig. 6b, page 47*), P1, K1 tbl, P1, YO, P2 tog, P6, K1 tbl; repeat from ★ once **more**, place marker, purl across to last 2 sts, K2.

Row 4 AND ALL WRONG SIDE ROWS: P2, knit across to next marker, P1 tbl (*Fig. B, page 45*), ★ (K9, P1 tbl) twice; repeat from ★ once **more**, knit across to last 2 sts, P2.

Row 5: K2, purl across to next marker, K1 tbl, ★ P5, P2 tog, YO, P2, K1 tbl, P2, YO, P2 tog, P5, K1 tbl; repeat from ★ once **more**, purl across to last 2 sts, K2.

Row 7: K2, purl across to next marker, K1 tbl, ★ P4, P2 tog, YO, P3, K1 tbl, P3, YO, P2 tog, P4, K1 tbl; repeat from ★ once **more**, purl across to last 2 sts, K2.

Row 9: K2, purl across to next marker, K1 tbl, ★ P3, P2 tog, YO, P4, K1 tbl, P4, YO, P2 tog, P3, K1 tbl; repeat from ★ once **more**, purl across to last 2 sts, K2.

Row 11: K2, purl across to next marker, K1 tbl, ★ P2, P2 tog, YO, P5, K1 tbl, P5, YO, P2 tog, P2, K1 tbl; repeat from ★ once **more**, purl across to last 2 sts, K2.

Row 13: K2, purl across to next marker, K1 tbl, ★ P1, P2 tog, YO, P6, K1 tbl, P6, YO, P2 tog, P1, K1 tbl; repeat from ★ once **more**, purl across to last 2 sts, K2.

Row 15: K2, purl across to next marker, K1 tbl, ★ P2 tog, YO, P7, K1 tbl, P7, YO, P2 tog, K1 tbl; repeat from ★ once **more**, purl across to last 2 sts, K2.

Row 17: K2, purl across to next marker, K1 tbl, ★ P1, YO, P2 tog, P6, K1 tbl, P6, P2 tog, YO, P1, K1 tbl; repeat from ★ once **more**, purl across to last 2 sts, K2.

Row 19: K2, purl across to next marker, K1 tbl, ★ P2, YO, P2 tog, P5, K1 tbl, P5, P2 tog, YO, P2, K1 tbl; repeat from ★ once **more**, purl across to last 2 sts, K2.

Row 21: K2, purl across to next marker, K1 tbl, ★ P3, YO, P2 tog, P4, K1 tbl, P4, P2 tog, YO, P3, K1 tbl; repeat from ★ once **more**, purl across to last 2 sts, K2.

Row 23: K2, purl across to next marker, K1 tbl, ★ P4, YO, P2 tog, P3, K1 tbl, P3, P2 tog, YO, P4, K1 tbl; repeat from ★ once **more**, purl across to last 2 sts, K2.

Row 25: K2, purl across to next marker, K1 tbl, ★ P5, YO, P2 tog, P2, K1 tbl, P2, P2 tog, YO, P5, K1 tbl; repeat from ★ once **more**, purl across to last 2 sts, K2.

Row 27: K2, purl across to next marker, K1 tbl, ★ P6, YO, P2 tog, P1, K1 tbl, P1, P2 tog, YO, P6, K1 tbl; repeat from ★ once **more**, purl across to last 2 sts, K2.

Row 29: K2, purl across to next marker, K1 tbl, ★ P7, YO, P2 tog, K1 tbl, P2 tog, YO, P7, K1 tbl; repeat from ★ once **more**, purl across to last 2 sts, K2.

Row 31: K2, purl across to next marker, K1 tbl, ★ P6, P2 tog, YO, P1, K1 tbl, P1, YO, P2 tog, P6, K1 tbl; repeat from ★ once **more**, purl across to last 2 sts, K2.

Repeat Rows 4-31 for pattern until piece measures approximately 15½" (39.5 cm) from cast on edge, ending by working Row 22.

ARMHOLE SHAPING

Maintain established pattern throughout and maintain 2 edge sts worked in Stockinette Stitch at **each** Armhole edge.

Rows 1 and 2: Bind off 4{5-6} sts, work across in pattern: 65{69-75} sts.

Instructions continued on page 16.

Row 3 (Decrease row): K1, SSK (*Figs. 3a-c, page 46*), work across in pattern to last 3 sts, K2 tog (*Fig. 1, page 46*), K1: 63{67-73} sts.

Row 4: Work across in pattern.

Rows 5 thru 9{11-15}: Repeat Rows 3 and 4, 2{3-5} times; then repeat Row 3 once **more**: 57{59-61} sts.

Work even until Armholes measure approximately 8{8½-9}"/20.5{21.5-23} cm, ending by working a **wrong** side row.

NECK & SHOULDER SHAPING
Row 1: Bind off 5 sts at Armhole edge, work across in pattern until there are 20{21-22} sts on the right needle, bind off next 7 sts, work in pattern across remaining sts.

Both sides of Neck are worked at the same time, using separate yarn for **each** side. Maintain established pattern throughout.

Row 2: Bind off 5 sts at Armhole edge, work across in pattern; with second yarn, bind off 5 sts at Neck edge, work across in pattern.

Rows 3 and 4: Bind off 5{5-6} sts at Armhole edge, work across in pattern; with second yarn, bind off 5 sts at Neck edge, work across in pattern.

Row 5: Bind off all sts on first side; with second yarn, bind off 5 sts at Neck edge, work across in pattern.

Bind off remaining sts.

FRONT
Cast on 73{79-87} sts.

Row 1 (Right side): Knit across.

Row 2: Purl across.

Beginning with Row 17{15-11}, work same as Back until Front measures approximately 19½{20-20½}"/49.5{51-52} cm, ending by working Row 28: 57{59-61} sts.

NECK SHAPING
Row 1 (Dividing row): Work in pattern across 28{29-30} sts, M1P (*Figs. 5a & b, page 47*), bind off next st, M1P, work across in pattern: 29{30-31} sts **each** side.

Both sides of Neck are worked at same time, using separate yarn for **each** side. Maintain established pattern throughout.

Row 2: Work across in pattern to within 2 sts of Neck edge, P2; with second yarn, P2, work across in pattern.

Row 3 (Decrease row): Work across in pattern to within 4 sts of Neck edge, P2 tog, K2; with second yarn, K2, P2 tog, work across: 28{29-30} sts each side.

Rows 4-29: Repeat Rows 2 and 3, 13 times: 15{16-17} sts each side.

Work even until Front measures same as Back to Shoulder Shaping, ending by working a **wrong** side row.

SHOULDER SHAPING
Rows 1 and 2: Bind off 5 sts at Armhole edge, work across in pattern; with second yarn, work across in pattern: 10{11-12} sts **each** side.

Rows 3 and 4: Bind off 5{5-6} sts at Armhole edge, work across in pattern; with second yarn, work across in pattern: 5{6-6} sts **each** side.

Row 5: Bind off all sts on first side; with second yarn, work across in pattern.

Bind off remaining sts.

SLEEVE (Make 2)
Cast on 31{31-33} sts.

Row 1: Knit across.

Row 2: Purl across.

Row 3 (Right side): K2, P3{3-4}, place marker, K1 tbl, P6, P2 tog, YO, P1, K1 tbl, P1, YO, P2 tog, P6, K1 tbl, place marker, P3{3-4}, K2.

Row 4 AND ALL WRONG SIDE ROWS: P2, knit across to next marker, P1 tbl, (K9, P1 tbl) twice, knit across to last 2 sts, P2.

Row 5: K2, purl across to next marker, K1 tbl, P5, P2 tog, YO, P2, K1 tbl, P2, YO, P2 tog, P5, K1 tbl, purl across to last 2 sts, K2.

Row 7: K2, purl across to next marker, K1 tbl, P4, P2 tog, YO, P3, K1 tbl, P3, YO, P2 tog, P4, K1 tbl, purl across to last 2 sts, K2.

Row 9 (Increase row): K2, M1P, purl across to next marker, K1 tbl, P3, P2 tog, YO, P4, K1 tbl, P4, YO, P2 tog, P3, K1 tbl, purl across to last 2 sts, M1P, K2: 33{33-35} sts.

Row 11: K2, purl across to next marker, K1 tbl, P2, P2 tog, YO, P5, K1 tbl, P5, YO, P2 tog, P2, K1 tbl, purl across to last 2 sts, K2.

Row 13: K2, purl across to next marker, K1 tbl, P1, P2 tog, YO, P6, K1 tbl, P6, YO, P2 tog, P1, K1 tbl, purl across to last 2 sts, K2.

Row 15: K2, purl across to next marker, K1 tbl, P2 tog, YO, P7, K1 tbl, P7, YO, P2 tog, K1 tbl, purl across to last 2 sts, K2.

Row 17 (Increase row): K2, M1P, purl across to next marker, K1 tbl, P1, YO, P2 tog, P6, K1 tbl, P6, P2 tog, YO, P1, K1 tbl, purl across to last 2 sts, M1P, K2: 35{35-37} sts.

Row 19: K2, purl across to next marker, K1 tbl, P2, YO, P2 tog, P5, K1 tbl, P5, P2 tog, YO, P2, K1 tbl, purl across to last 2 sts, K2.

Row 21: K2, purl across to next marker, K1 tbl, P3, YO, P2 tog, P4, K1 tbl, P4, P2 tog, YO, P3, K1 tbl, purl across to last 2 sts, K2.

Row 23: K2, purl across to next marker, K1 tbl, P4, YO, P2 tog, P3, K1 tbl, P3, P2 tog, YO, P4, K1 tbl, purl across to last 2 sts, K2.

Row 25 (Increase row): K2, M1P, purl across to next marker, K1 tbl, P5, YO, P2 tog, P2, K1 tbl, P2, P2 tog, YO, P5, K1 tbl, purl across to last 2 sts, M1P, K2: 37{37-39} sts.

Row 27: K2, purl across to next marker, K1 tbl, P6, YO, P2 tog, P1, K1 tbl, P1, P2 tog, YO, P6, K1 tbl, purl across to last 2 sts, K2.

Row 29: K2, purl across to next marker, K1 tbl, P7, YO, P2 tog, K1 tbl, P2 tog, YO, P7, K1 tbl, purl across to last 2 sts, K2.

Row 31: K2, purl across to next marker, K1 tbl, P6, P2 tog, YO, P1, K1 tbl, P1, YO, P2 tog, P6, K1 tbl, purl across to last 2 sts, K2.

Working established pattern between markers (Rows 4-31), continue to increase one stitch at **each** edge in same manner, every 8th row, 7{6-3} times; then increase, every 6th row, 0{2-6} times *(see Zeros, page 44)*: 51{53-57} sts.

Work even until Sleeve measures approximately 17½{18-18}"/44.5{45.5-45.5} cm from cast on edge, ending by working a **wrong** side row.

SLEEVE CAP
Maintain established pattern throughout.

Rows 1 and 2: Bind off 4{5-6} sts, work across in pattern: 43{43-45} sts.

Row 3 (Decrease row): K1, SSK, work across to last 3 sts, K2 tog, K1: 41{41-43} sts.

Row 4: Work across in pattern.

Rows 5 thru 28{28-30}: Repeat Rows 3 and 4, 12{12-13} times: 17 sts.

Last 2 Rows: Bind off 2 sts, work across in pattern: 13 sts.

Bind off remaining sts.

FINISHING
BACK NECK TRIM
With **right** side facing, pick up one stitch in each stitch across back neck edge *(Figs. 8a & b, page 48)*.

Row 1: Knit across.

Row 2: Purl across.

Bind off all sts in **knit**.

Sew shoulder seams, joining edge of Back Neck Trim to front V-Neck where they meet.

Sew Sleeves into armholes matching bound off sts at underarm and placing center of Cap at shoulder seam.

Weave underarm and side in one continuous seam *(Fig. 9, page 48)*.

You've just found your new weekend **favorite**! The appealing texture is enhanced by the **thickness** of bulky weight yarn. And the neutral color of this cardigan will partner well with all your casual separates.

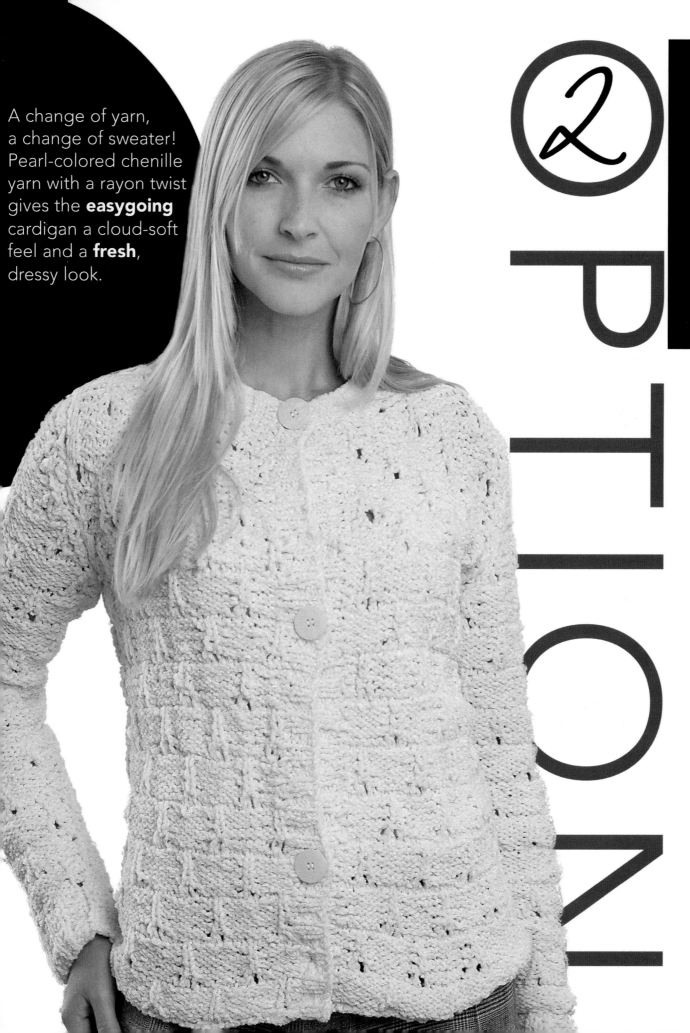

A change of yarn, a change of sweater! Pearl-colored chenille yarn with a rayon twist gives the **easygoing** cardigan a cloud-soft feel and a **fresh**, dressy look.

OPTION
2

Option 1

Reynolds® Cabana
Bulky Weight Yarn

BULKY 5

   [3$\frac{1}{2}$ ounces, 135 yards
   (100 grams, 123 meters) per skein]:
   #950 Wheat - 8{9-10} skeins
32" (81 cm) Circular knitting needles,
   sizes 9 (5.5 mm) **and** 10 (6 mm) **or**
   sizes needed for gauge
Straight knitting needles, size 10 (6 mm) **or**
   size needed for gauge
Yarn needle
1$\frac{1}{4}$" (32 mm) Buttons - 3

GAUGE: With larger size needles,
        in Stockinette Stitch,
        14 sts and 20 rows = 4" (10 cm)
        in pattern,
        15 sts and 22 rows = 4" (10 cm)

RELAXED & HAPPY   ⬛⬛⬛⬜ INTERMEDIATE

Option 2

Caron® Jewelbox™
Bulky Weight Yarn

BULKY 5

   [2$\frac{1}{2}$ ounces, 90 yards
   (70.9 grams, 83 meters) per skein]:
   #0001 Pearl - 10{12-13} skeins
32" (81 cm) Circular knitting needles,
   sizes 9 (5.5 mm) **and** 10 (6 mm) **or**
   sizes needed for gauge
Straight knitting needles, size 10 (6 mm) **or**
   size needed for gauge
Yarn needle
1$\frac{1}{4}$" (32 mm) Buttons - 3

GAUGE: With larger size needles,
        in Stockinette Stitch,
        14 sts and 20 rows = 4" (10 cm)
        in pattern,
        15 sts and 22 rows = 4" (10 cm)

Size	Finished Chest Measurement
Small	39$\frac{1}{2}$" (100.5 cm)
Medium	43$\frac{3}{4}$" (111 cm)
Large	48" (122 cm)

Size Note: Instructions are written for size Small with sizes Medium and Large in braces { }. Instructions will be easier to read if you circle all the numbers pertaining to your size. If only one number is given, it applies to all sizes.

BODY

With smaller size needle, cast on 146{162-178} sts.

Row 1 (Right side)**:** Knit across.

Row 2: Purl across.

Row 3: K1, ★ YO *(Figs. 6b & c, page 47)*, P2 tog *(Fig. 2, page 46)*, P6; repeat from ★ across to last st, K1.

Row 4: (P1, K7) across to last 2 sts, P2.

Row 5: K2, (P7, K1) across.

Rows 6-9: Repeat Rows 4 and 5 twice.

Row 10: Purl across.

Change to larger size circular needle.

Row 11: K1, P4, YO, P2 tog, (P6, YO, P2 tog) across to last 3 sts, P2, K1.

Row 12: P1, K3, P1, (K7, P1) across to last 5 sts, K4, P1.

Row 13: K1, P4, K1, (P7, K1) across to last 4 sts, P3, K1.

Rows 14-17: Repeat Rows 12 and 13 twice.

Row 18: Purl across.

Row 19: K1, (YO, P2 tog, P6) across to last st, K1.

Row 20: (P1, K7) across to last 2 sts, P2.

Row 21: K2, (P7, K1) across.

Rows 22-25: Repeat Rows 20 and 21 twice.

Row 26: Purl across.

Repeat Rows 11-26 for pattern until Body measures approximately 14$\frac{1}{2}$" (37 cm) from cast on edge, ending by working a **right** side row.

Dividing Row: Maintain established pattern, work across first 32{36-39} sts (Left Front), bind off next 8{8-10} sts (armhole), work across next 65{73-79} sts (Back), bind off next 8{8-10} sts (armhole), work across last 31{35-38} sts (Right Front): 130{146-158} sts [32{36-39} sts **each** for Left & Right Front and 66{74-80} sts for Back].

RIGHT FRONT

Maintain established pattern throughout, working one edge stitch at front edge and 2 edge stitches at armhole edge.

Row 1 (Right side)**:** With straight needles, K1 (edge stitch), work in pattern across next 28{32-35} sts, K2 tog *(Fig. 1, page 46)*, K1; leave remaining sts on circular needle: 31{35-38} sts.

Row 2: P2 (edge stitches), work in pattern across to last st, P1.

Row 3 (Decrease row)**:** K1, work in pattern across to last 3 sts, K2 tog, K1: 30{34-37} sts.

Rows 4 thru 7{11-13}: Repeat Rows 2 and 3, 2{4-5} times: 28{30-32} sts.

Work even until Armhole measures approximately 6$\frac{1}{4}${6$\frac{3}{4}$-7$\frac{1}{4}$}"/16{17-18.5} cm, ending by working a **wrong** side row.

Instructions continued on page 22.

NECK SHAPING
Row 1: Bind off 4 sts, work in pattern across to last 2 sts, K2: 24{26-28} sts.

Row 2: P2, work across in pattern.

Rows 3 and 4: Repeat Rows 1 and 2: 20{22-24} sts.

Row 5: Bind off 3{3-4} sts, work in pattern across to last 2 sts, K2: 17{19-20} sts.

Row 6: P2, work across in pattern.

Row 7: Bind off 3 sts, work in pattern across to last 2 sts, K2: 14{16-17} sts.

Work even in pattern until Armhole measures approximately 8$^1/_4${8$^3/_4$-8$^1/_4$"/21{22-23.5} cm, ending by working a **right** side row.

SHOULDER SHAPING
Row 1: Bind off 4{5-5} sts, work across in pattern: 10{11-12} sts.

Row 2: Work across in pattern.

Row 3: Bind off 5{5-6} sts, work across in pattern: 5{6-6} sts.

Row 4: Work across in pattern.

Bind off remaining sts.

BACK
Maintain established pattern throughout, working 2 edge stitches at each Armhole edge.

Row 1 (Right side)**:** With **right** side of Body facing and using straight needles, K1, SSK *(Figs. 3a-c, page 46)*, work in pattern across next 60{68-74} sts, K2 tog, K1, leave remaining sts on circular needle: 64{72-78} sts.

Row 2: P2, work across in pattern to last 2 sts, P2.

Row 3 (Decrease row)**:** K1, SSK, work across in pattern to last 3 sts, K2 tog, K1: 62{70-76} sts.

Rows 4 thru 7{11-13}: Repeat Rows 2 and 3, 2{4-5} times: 58{62-66} sts.

Work even in pattern until Armholes measure approximately 8$^1/_4${8$^3/_4$-9$^1/_4$"/21{22-23.5} cm, ending by working a **wrong** side row.

NECK & SHOULDER SHAPING
Row 1: Bind off 4{5-5} sts, work in pattern across next 19{20-21} sts, bind off next 10{10-12} sts, work across in pattern to last 2 sts, K2.

Both sides of Neck are worked at same time, using separate yarn for **each** side.

Row 2: Bind off 4{5-5} sts at Armhole edge, work across in pattern; with second yarn, bind off 5 sts at Neck edge, work across in pattern.

Rows 3 and 4: Bind off 5{5-6} sts at Armhole edge, work across in pattern; with second yarn, bind off 5 sts at Neck edge, work across in pattern.

Row 5: Bind off all sts on first side; with second yarn, bind off 5 sts at neck edge, work across in pattern.

Bind off remaining sts.

LEFT FRONT
Maintain established pattern throughout, working one edge stitch at front edge and 2 edge stitches at Armhole edge.

Row 1 (Right side)**:** With **right** side facing and using straight needles, K1, SSK, work across in pattern to last st, K1: 31{35-38} sts.

Row 2: P1, work across in pattern to last 2 sts, P2.

Row 3 (Decrease row)**:** K1, SSK, work across in pattern to last st, K1: 30{34-37} sts.

Rows 4 thru 7{11-13}: Repeat Rows 2 and 3, 2{4-5} times: 28{30-32} sts.

Work even until Armhole measures approximately 6$^1/_4${6$^3/_4$-7$^1/_4$"/16{17-18.5} cm, ending by working a **right** side row.

NECK SHAPING
Row 1: Bind off 4 sts, work across in pattern to last 2 sts, P2: 24{26-28} sts.

Row 2: K2, work across in pattern.

Rows 3 and 4: Repeat Rows 1 and 2: 20{22-24} sts.

Row 5: Bind off 3{3-4} sts, work across in pattern to last 2 sts, P2: 17{19-20} sts.

Row 6: K2, work across in pattern.

Row 7: Bind off 3 sts, work across in pattern to last 2 sts, P2: 14{16-17} sts.

Work even until Armhole measures approximately 8¼{8¾-9¼}"/21{22-23.5} cm, ending by working a **wrong** side row.

SHOULDER SHAPING

Row 1: Bind off 4{5-5} sts, work across in pattern: 10{11-12} sts.

Row 2: Work across in pattern.

Row 3: Bind off 5{5-6} sts, work across in pattern: 5{6-6} sts.

Row 4: Work across in pattern.

Bind off remaining sts.

SLEEVE (Make 2)
RIBBING

With smaller size needles, cast on 45 sts.

Row 1 (Right side)**:** K3, (P3, K3) across.

Row 2: P3, (K3, P3) across.

Repeat Rows 1 and 2 until Ribbing measures approximately 2¼" (5.5 cm), ending by working Row 1.

Next Row: Purl across decreasing 9 sts evenly spaced (*see Decreasing Evenly Across A Row, page 45*): 36 sts.

BODY
Change to larger size needles.

Row 1 (Right side)**:** K2, (YO, P2 tog, P6) across to last 2 sts, K2.
Row 2: P2, K7, (P1, K7) across to last 3 sts, P3.

Row 3: K3, P7, (K1, P7) across to last 2 sts, K2.

Row 4: P2, K7, (P1, K7) across to last 3 sts, P3.

Row 5 (Increase row)**:** K2, M1 (*Figs. 4a & b, page 46*), K1, P7, (K1, P7) across to last 2 sts, M1, K2: 38 sts.

Row 6: P3, (K7, P1) across to last 3 sts, K1, P2.

Row 7: K2, P1, (K1, P7) across to last 3 sts, K3.

Row 8: Purl across.

Row 9: K2, P5, YO, P2 tog, (P6, YO, P2 tog) across to last 5 sts, P3, K2.

Row 10: P2, K4, P1, (K7, P1) across to last 7 sts, K5, P2.

Row 11: K2, P5, K1, (P7, K1) across to last 6 sts, P4, K2.

Row 12: P2, K4, P1, (K7, P1) across to last 7 sts, K5, P2.

Row 13 (Increase row)**:** K2, M1, P5, K1, (P7, K1) across to last 6 sts, P4, M1, K2: 40 sts.

Row 14: P2, K5, P1, (K7, P1) across to last 8 sts, K6, P2.

Row 15: K2, P6, K1, (P7, K1) across to last 7 sts, P5, K2.

Row 16: Purl across.

Row 17: K2, P2, YO, P2 tog, (P6, YO, P2 tog) across to last 2 sts, K2.

Row 18: P2, K1, P1, (K7, P1) across to last 4 sts, K2, P2.

Instructions continued on page 24.

Row 19: K2, P2, K1, (P7, K1) across to last 3 sts, P1, K2.

Row 20: P2, K1, P1, (K7, P1) across to last 4 sts, K2, P2.

Row 21 (Increase row)**:** K2, M1, P2, K1, (P7, K1) across to last 3 sts, P1, M1, K2: 42 sts.

Continuing in established pattern and working new sts in pattern, continue to increase one stitch at **each** edge in same manner, every 8th row, 2{5-9} times **more**; then increase every 10th row, 5{3-0} times (*see Zeros, page 44*): 56{58-60} sts.

Work even until Sleeve measures approximately 17$\frac{1}{2}${18-18}"/44.5{45.5-45.5} cm from cast on edge, ending by working a **wrong** side row.

SLEEVE CAP
Maintain established pattern throughout.

Rows 1 and 2: Bind off 4{4-5} sts, work across in pattern: 48{50-50} sts.

Row 3 (Decrease row)**:** K1, SSK, work across in pattern to last 3 sts, K2 tog, K1: 46{48-48} sts.

Row 4: P2, work across in pattern to last 2 sts, P2.

Rows 5 thru 28{32-30}: Repeat Rows 3 and 4, 12{14-13} times: 22{20-22} sts.

Next 4{2-6} Rows: Bind off 2{3-2} sts, work across in pattern: 14{14-10} sts.

Bind off remaining sts.

FINISHING
Sew shoulder seams.

Weave Sleeve seams (*Fig. 9, page 48*).

Sew Sleeves into armholes matching bound off sts at underarm and placing center of Cap at shoulder seam.

NECK RIBBING
With **right** side facing and using smaller size needle, pick up 92 sts evenly spaced around entire Neck edge (*Figs. 8a & b, page 48*).

Row 1: P3, K2, (P2, K2) across to last 3 sts, P3.

Row 2 (Right side)**:** K3, P2, (K2, P2) across to last 3 sts, K3.

Repeat Rows 1 and 2 until Neck Ribbing measures approximately 1$\frac{1}{4}$" (3 cm), ending by working Row 1.

Bind off all sts in pattern.

LEFT FRONT BAND
With **right** side facing and using smaller size needle, pick up 90{94-94} sts evenly spaced along Left Front edge.

Row 1: P2, (K2, P2) across.

Row 2 (Right side)**:** K2, (P2, K2) across.

Rows 3-6: Repeat Rows 1 and 2 twice.

Bind off all sts in pattern.

RIGHT FRONT BAND

With **right** side facing and using smaller size needle, pick up 90{94-94} sts evenly spaced along Right Front edge.

Row 1: P2, (K2, P2) across.

Row 2 (Right side)**:** K2, (P2, K2) across.

Row 3 (Buttonhole row)**:** P2, bind off next 3 sts (buttonhole), ★ (K2, P2) 7 times, bind off next 3 sts (buttonhole); repeat from ★ once **more**, (K2, P2) 5{6-6} times: 81{85-85} sts.

Row 4: (K2, P2) 5{6-6} times, K1, **turn**; add on 3 sts *(Figs. 7a & b, page 48)*, **turn**; ★ (K2, P2) 7 times, K1, **turn**; add on 3 sts, **turn**; repeat from ★ once **more**, K2: 90{94-94} sts.

Rows 5 and 6: Repeat Rows 1 and 2.

Bind off all sts in pattern.

Sew buttons to Left Front Band opposite buttonholes.

OPTION 1

Perhaps we should call this cropped cardigan "Short and Sweet." The **soft** lavender yarn is feminine and comfortable, and the ribbed body provides a **gentle** contrast to the smooth sleeves.

On the other hand, "Saucy" is the word that fits this **sensational** sweater. It may be short in length, but it is definitely long on **spunk**. Wear the irrepressibly pink cardigan and add a little more pizzazz to your day.

OPTION ②

Option 1

Reynolds Yarns Saucy Sport
Light/Worsted Weight Yarn
  [1³/₄ ounces, 123 yards
  (50 grams, 112 meters) per skein]:
  #138 Iris - 9{11-13} skeins
Straight knitting needles, sizes 3 (3.25 mm) **and**
  5 (3.75 mm) **or** sizes needed for gauge
Markers
Yarn needle
¹/₂" (12 mm) Buttons - 7

GAUGE: With larger size needles,
        in Reverse Stockinette Stitch,
        24 sts and 32 rows = 4" (10 cm)
        in pattern,
        30 sts and 32 rows = 4" (10 cm)

SHORT & SAUCY   ████▢ INTERMEDIATE

Option 2

Red Heart® Luster Sheen®
Light/Worsted Weight Yarn
  [4 ounces, 335 yards
  (110 grams, 306 meters) per skein]:
  #735 Hot Pink - 4{4-5} skeins
Straight knitting needles, sizes 3 (3.25 mm) **and**
  5 (3.75 mm) **or** sizes needed for gauge
Markers
Yarn needle
¹/₂" (12 mm) Buttons - 7

GAUGE: With larger size needles,
        in Reverse Stockinette Stitch,
        24 sts and 32 rows = 4" (10 cm)
        in pattern,
        30 sts and 32 rows = 4" (10 cm)

Size	Finished Chest Measurement
Small	38¹/₂" (98 cm)
Medium	43" (109 cm)
Large	47¹/₂" (120.5 cm)

Size Note: Instructions are written for size Small with sizes Medium and Large in braces { }. Instructions will be easier to read if you circle all the numbers pertaining to your size. If only one number is given, it applies to all sizes.

STITCH GUIDE

RIGHT TWIST (*abbreviated RT*) (uses 2 sts)
Working in **front** of first st on left needle, knit second st (*Fig. A*) making sure **not** to drop off, then knit into the back of first st (*Fig. B*) letting both sts drop off needle.

Fig. A

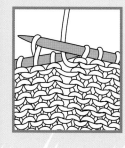

Fig. B

PATTERN STITCH

Row 1 (Right side): P2, K2, P2, K1, P1, K1, P3, P2 tog (*Fig. 2, page 46*), YO (*Fig. 6d, page 47*), ★ (K2, P2) twice, K1, P1, K1, P3, P2 tog, YO; repeat from ★ across.
Row 2: K5, P1, K1, P1, K2, P2, K2, ★ P2, K5, P1, K1, P1, K2, P2, K2; repeat from ★ across.
Row 3: P2, RT, P2, K1, P1, K1, P2, P2 tog, YO (*Fig. 6b, page 47*), P1, ★ K2, P2, RT, P2, K1, P1, K1, P2, P2 tog, YO, P1; repeat from ★ across.
Row 4: K5, P1, K1, P1, K2, P2, K2, ★ P2, K5, P1, K1, P1, K2, P2, K2; repeat from ★ across.
Row 5: P2, K2, P2, (K1, P1) twice, P2 tog, YO, P2, ★ (K2, P2) twice, (K1, P1) twice, P2 tog, YO, P2; repeat from ★ across.

Row 6: K5, P1, K1, P1, K2, P2, K2, ★ P2, K5, P1, K1, P1, K2, P2, K2; repeat from ★ across.
Row 7: P2, RT, P2, K1, P1, K1, P2 tog, YO, P3, ★ K2, P2, RT, P2, K1, P1, K1, P2 tog, YO, P3; repeat from ★ across.
Row 8: K5, P1, K1, P1, K2, P2, K2, ★ P2, K5, P1, K1, P1, K2, P2, K2; repeat from ★ across.
Row 9: P2, K2, (P1, K1) 3 times, P4, ★ K2, P2, K2, (P1, K1) 3 times, P4; repeat from ★ across.
Row 10: K4, (P1, K1) 3 times, P2, K2, ★ P2, K4, (P1, K1) 3 times, P2, K2; repeat from ★ across.
Row 11: P2, RT, (P1, K1) 3 times, P4, ★ K2, P2, RT, (P1, K1) 3 times, P4; repeat from ★ across.
Row 12: K4, (P1, K1) 3 times, P2, K2, ★ P2, K4, (P1, K1) 3 times, P2, K2; repeat from ★ across.
Row 13: P2, K2, (P1, K1) 3 times, P4, ★ K2, P2, K2, (P1, K1) 3 times, P4; repeat from ★ across.
Row 14: K4, (P1, K1) 3 times, P2, K2, ★ P2, K4, (P1, K1) 3 times, P2, K2; repeat from ★ across.
Row 15: P2, RT, (P1, K1) 3 times, P4, ★ K2, P2, RT, (P1, K1) 3 times, P4; repeat from ★ across.
Row 16: K4, (P1, K1) 3 times, P2, K2, ★ P2, K4, (P1, K1) 3 times, P2, K2; repeat from ★ across.
Repeat Rows 1-16 for pattern.

BACK
RIBBING

With smaller size needles, cast on 137{153-169} sts.

Row 1: P2, K1, (P1, K1) across to last 2 sts, P2.

Row 2 (Right side): K2, P1, (K1, P1) across to last 2 sts, K2.

Repeat Rows 1 and 2 until Ribbing measures approximately ¹/₂" (12 mm), ending by working Row 2.

Decrease Row: Purl across decreasing 7 sts evenly spaced (*see Decreasing Evenly Across A Row, page 45*): 130{146-162} sts.

Instructions continued on page 30.

BODY

Change to larger size needles.

Row 1 (Right side): K2, place marker *(see Markers, page 44)*, work Row 1 of Pattern Stitch across to last 2 sts, place marker, K2.

Row 2: P2, slip marker, work next row of Pattern Stitch across to next marker, slip marker, P2.

Row 3: K2, slip marker, work next row of Pattern Stitch across to next marker, slip marker, K2.

Row 4: P2, slip marker, work next row of Pattern Stitch across to next marker, slip marker, P2.

Row 5 (Increase row): K2, M1 *(Figs. 4a & b, page 46)*, slip marker, work next row of Pattern Stitch across to next marker, slip marker, M1, K2: 132{148-164} sts.

Continuing in Pattern Stitch, work M1 increase **before** first marker and **after** second marker, every 8th row, 7 times working increase sts in K2, P2 rib; remove markers: 146{162-178} sts.

Work even until Back measures approximately 8$\frac{1}{2}$" (21.5 cm) from cast on edge, ending by working a **wrong** side row.

ARMHOLE SHAPING

Maintain established pattern throughout.

Rows 1 and 2: Bind off 8{10-12} sts, work across in Pattern Stitch: 130{142-154} sts.

Rows 3 and 4: Bind off 2{3-3} sts, work across in Pattern Stitch: 126{136-148} sts.

Row 5 (Decrease row): K1, SSK *(Figs. 3a-c, page 46)*, work across in Pattern Stitch to last 3 sts, K2 tog *(Fig. 1, page 46)*, K1: 124{134-146} sts.

Row 6: P2, work across in Pattern Stitch to last 2 sts, P2.

Repeat Rows 5 and 6, 5{6-8} times: 114{122-130} sts.

Working 2 edge sts in Stockinette Stitch at **each** Armhole edge, work even until Armholes measure approximately 8$\frac{1}{4}${8$\frac{3}{4}$-9$\frac{1}{4}$}"/21{22-23.5} cm, ending by working a **wrong** side row.

NECK & SHOULDER SHAPING

Row 1: Bind off 9{10-11} sts at Armhole edge, work across in Pattern Stitch until there are 30{32-34} sts on right needle, bind off next 36{38-40} sts, work across in Pattern Stitch.

Both sides of Neck are worked at same time, using separate yarn for **each** side.

Row 2: Bind off 9{10-11} sts at Armhole edge, work across in Pattern Stitch; with second yarn, bind off 5 sts at Neck edge, work across in Pattern Stitch.

Rows 3 and 4: Bind off 10{11-12} sts at Armhole edge, work across in Pattern Stitch; with second yarn, bind off 5 sts at Neck edge, work across in Pattern Stitch.

Row 5: Bind off all sts on first side; with second yarn, bind off 5 sts at Neck edge, work across in Pattern Stitch.

Bind off remaining sts.

LEFT FRONT
RIBBING

With smaller size needles, cast on 71{79-87} sts.

Row 1: P2, K1, (P1, K1) across to last 2 sts, P2.

Row 2 (Right side): K2, P1, (K1, P1) across to last 2 sts, K2.

Repeat Rows 1 and 2 until Ribbing measures approximately $\frac{1}{2}$" (12 mm), ending by working Row 2.

Decrease Row: Purl across decreasing 5 sts evenly spaced: 66{74-82} sts.

BODY
Change to larger size needles.

SIZES SMALL & LARGE ONLY
Row 1 (Right side): K2, place marker, work Row 1 of Pattern Stitch across to last 2 sts, place marker, K2.

Row 2: P2, slip marker, work next row of Pattern Stitch across to next marker, slip marker, P2.

Row 3: K2, slip marker, work next row of Pattern Stitch across to next marker, slip marker, K2.

Row 4: P2, slip marker, work next row of Pattern Stitch across to next marker, slip marker, P2.

Row 5 (Increase row): K2, M1, slip marker, work next row of Pattern Stitch across to next marker, slip marker, K2: 67{83} sts.

Continuing in Pattern Stitch, work M1 increase **before** first marker, every 8th row, 7 times working increase sts in K2, P2 rib; remove markers: 74{90} sts.

Work even until Left Front measures approximately 8 1/2" (21.5 cm) from cast on edge, ending by working a **wrong** side row.

SIZE MEDIUM ONLY
Row 1 (Right side): K2, place marker, K1, P1, K1, P3, P2 tog, YO, work Row 1 of Pattern Stitch across to last 2 sts, place marker, K2.

Row 2: P2, slip marker, work next row of Pattern Stitch across to within 8 sts of next marker, K5, P1, K1, P1, slip marker, P2.

Row 3: K2, slip marker, K1, P1, K1, P2, P2 tog, YO, P1, work next row of Pattern Stitch across to next marker, slip marker, K2.

Row 4: P2, slip marker, work next row of Pattern Stitch across to within 8 sts of next marker, K5, P1, K1, P1, slip marker, P2.

Row 5 (Increase row): K2, M1, slip marker, (K1, P1) twice, P2 tog, YO, P2, work next row of Pattern Stitch across to next marker, slip marker, K2: {75} sts.

Row 6: P2, slip marker, work next row of Pattern Stitch across to within 8 sts of next marker, K5, P1, K1, P1, slip marker, P3.

Row 7: K3, slip marker, K1, P1, K1, P2 tog, YO, P3, work next row of Pattern Stitch across to next marker, slip marker, K2.

Row 8: P2, slip marker, work next row of Pattern Stitch across to within 8 sts of next marker, K5, P1, K1, P1, slip marker, P3.

Row 9: K3, slip marker, (P1, K1) twice, P4, work next row of Pattern Stitch across to next marker, slip marker, K2.

Row 10: P2, slip marker, work next row of Pattern Stitch across to within 8 sts of next marker, K4, (P1, K1) twice, slip marker, P3.

Rows 11 and 12: Repeat Rows 9 and 10.

Row 13 (Increase row): K3, M1, slip marker, (P1, K1) twice, P4, work next row of Pattern Stitch across to next marker, slip marker, K2: {76} sts.

Row 14: P2, slip marker, work next row of Pattern Stitch across to within 8 sts of next marker, K4, (P1, K1) twice, slip marker, P4.

Row 15: K4, slip marker, (P1, K1) twice, P4, work next row of Pattern Stitch across to next marker, slip marker, K2.

Row 16: P2, slip marker, work next row of Pattern Stitch across to within 8 sts of next marker, K4, (P1, K1) twice, slip marker, P4.

Continuing in Pattern Stitch, work M1 increase **before** first marker, every 8th row, 6 times **more** working increase sts in K2, P2 rib; remove markers: {82} sts.

Work even until Left Front measures approximately 8 1/2" (21.5 cm) from cast on edge, ending by working a **wrong** side row.

Instructions continued on page 32.

ARMHOLE SHAPING - ALL SIZES
Maintain established pattern throughout.

Row 1: Bind off 8{10-12} sts, work across in Pattern Stitch: 66{72-78} sts.

Row 2: Work across in Pattern Stitch.

Rows 3: Bind off 2{3-3} sts, work across in Pattern Stitch: 64{69-75} sts.

Row 4: Work across in Pattern Stitch.

Row 5 (Decrease row): K1, SSK, work across in Pattern Stitch: 63{68-74} sts.

Row 6: Work across in Pattern Stitch.

Repeat Rows 5 and 6, 5{6-8} times: 58{62-66} sts.

Working 2 edge sts in Stockinette Stitch at **each** edge, work even until Armhole measures approximately $6^{1}/_{4}${$6^{3}/_{4}$-$7^{1}/_{4}$}"/ 16{17-18.5} cm, ending by working a **right** side row.

NECK SHAPING
Row 1: Bind off 9 sts, work across in Pattern Stitch: 49{53-57} sts.

Row 2: Work across in Pattern Stitch.

Row 3: Bind off 4{5-5} sts, work across in Pattern Stitch: 45{48-52} sts.

Row 4: Work across in Pattern Stitch.

Row 5: Bind off 4{4-5} sts, work across in Pattern Stitch: 41{44-47} sts.

Row 6: Work across in Pattern Stitch.

Row 7: Bind off 4 sts, work across in Pattern Stitch: 37{40-43} sts.

Rows 8-11: Repeat Rows 6 and 7 twice: 29{32-35} sts.

Work even until Armhole measures approximately $8^{1}/_{4}${$8^{3}/_{4}$-$9^{1}/_{4}$}"/21{22-23.5} cm, ending by working a **wrong** side row.

SHOULDER SHAPING
Row 1: Bind off 9{10-11} sts, work across in Pattern Stitch: 20{22-24} sts.

Row 2: Work across in Pattern Stitch.

Row 3: Bind off 10{11-12} sts, work across in Pattern Stitch: 10{11-12} sts.

Row 4: Work across in Pattern Stitch.

Bind off remaining sts.

RIGHT FRONT
RIBBING
With smaller size needles, cast on 71{79-87} sts.

Row 1: P2, K1, (P1, K1) across to last 2 sts, P2.

Row 2 (Right side): K2, P1, (K1, P1) across to last 2 sts, K2.

Repeat Rows 1 and 2 until Ribbing measures approximately $^{1}/_{2}$" (12 mm), ending by working Row 2.

Decrease Row: Purl across decreasing 5 sts evenly spaced: 66{74-82} sts.

BODY
Change to larger size needles.

SIZES SMALL & LARGE ONLY
Row 1 (Right side): K2, place marker, work Row 1 of Pattern Stitch across to last 2 sts, place marker, K2.

Row 2: P2, slip marker, work next row of Pattern Stitch across to next marker, slip marker, P2.

Row 3: K2, slip marker, work next row of Pattern Stitch across to next marker, slip marker, K2.

Row 4: P2, slip marker, work next row of Pattern Stitch across to next marker, slip marker, P2.

Row 5 (Increase row): K2, slip marker, work next row of Pattern Stitch across to next marker, slip marker, M1, K2: 67{83} sts.

Continuing in Pattern Stitch, work M1 increase **after** second marker, every 8th row, 7 times working increase sts in K2, P2 rib; remove markers: 74{90} sts.

Work even until Left Front measures approximately 8½" (21.5 cm) from cast on edge, ending by working a **right** side row.

SIZE MEDIUM ONLY

Row 1 (Right side): K2, place marker, work Row 1 of Pattern Stitch across to last 10 sts, (K2, P2) twice, place marker, K2.

Row 2: P2, slip marker, (K2, P2) twice, work next row of Pattern Stitch across to next marker, slip marker, P2.

Row 3: K2, slip marker, work next row of Pattern Stitch across to within 8 sts of next marker, K2, P2, RT, P2, slip marker, K2.

Row 4: P2, slip marker, (K2, P2) twice, work next row of Pattern Stitch across to next marker, slip marker, P2.

Row 5 (Increase row): K2, slip marker, work next row of Pattern Stitch across to within 8 sts of next marker, (K2, P2) twice, slip marker, M1, K2: {75} sts.

Row 6: P3, slip marker, (K2, P2) twice, work next row of Pattern Stitch across to next marker, slip marker, P2.

Row 7: K2, slip marker, work next row of Pattern Stitch across to within 8 sts of next marker, K2, P2, RT, P2, slip marker, K3.

Row 8: P3, slip marker, (K2, P2) twice, work next row of Pattern Stitch across to next marker, slip marker, P2.

Row 9: K2, slip marker, work next row of Pattern Stitch across to within 8 sts of next marker, K2, P2, K2, P1, K1, slip marker, K3.

Row 10: P3, slip marker, P1, K1, P2, K2, P2, work next row of Pattern Stitch across to next marker, slip marker, P2.

Row 11: K2, slip marker, work next row of Pattern Stitch across to within 8 sts of next marker, K2, P2, RT, P1, K1, slip marker, K3.

Row 12: P3, slip marker, P1, K1, P2, K2, P2, work next row of Pattern Stitch across to next marker, slip marker, P2.

Row 13 (Increase row): K2, slip marker, work next row of Pattern Stitch across to within 8 sts of next marker, K2, P2, K2, P1, K1, slip marker, M1, K3: {76} sts.

Row 14: P4, slip marker, P1, K1, P2, K2, P2, work next row of Pattern Stitch across to next marker, slip marker, P2.

Row 15: K2, slip marker, work next row of Pattern Stitch across to within 8 sts of next marker, K2, P2, RT, P1, K1, slip marker, K4.

Row 16: P4, slip marker, P1, K1, P2, K2, P2, work next row of Pattern Stitch across to next marker, slip marker, P4.

Continuing in Pattern Stitch, work M1 increase **after** second marker, every 8th row, 6 times **more** working increase sts in K2, P2 rib; remove markers: {82} sts.

Work even until Left Front measures approximately 8½" (21.5 cm) from cast on edge, ending by working a **right** side row.

ARMHOLE SHAPING - ALL SIZES
Maintain established pattern throughout.

Row 1: Bind off 8{10-12} sts, work across in Pattern Stitch: 66{72-78} sts.

Row 2: Work across in Pattern Stitch.

Rows 3: Bind off 2{3-3} sts, work across in Pattern Stitch: 64{69-75} sts.

Row 4: Work across in Pattern Stitch.

Instructions continued on page 34.

Row 5 (Decrease row): K1, SSK, work across in Pattern Stitch: 63{68-74} sts.

Row 6: Work across in Pattern Stitch.

Repeat Rows 5 and 6, 5{6-8} times: 58{62-66} sts.

Working 2 edge sts in Stockinette Stitch at **each** edge, work even until Armhole measures approximately 6$\frac{1}{4}${6$\frac{3}{4}$-7$\frac{1}{4}$}"/ 16{17-18.5} cm, ending by working a **wrong** side row.

NECK SHAPING
Row 1: Bind off 9 sts, work across in Pattern Stitch: 49{53-57} sts.

Row 2: Work across in Pattern Stitch.

Row 3: Bind off 4{5-5} sts, work across in Pattern Stitch: 45{48-52} sts.

Row 4: Work across in Pattern Stitch.

Row 5: Bind off 4{4-5} sts, work across in Pattern Stitch: 41{44-47} sts.

Row 6: Work across in Pattern Stitch.

Row 7: Bind off 4 sts, work across in Pattern Stitch: 37{40-43} sts.

Rows 8-11: Repeat Rows 6 and 7 twice: 29{32-35} sts.

Work even until Armhole measures approximately 8$\frac{1}{4}${8$\frac{3}{4}$-9$\frac{1}{4}$}"/21{22-23.5} cm, ending by working a **right** side row.

SHOULDER SHAPING
Row 1: Bind off 9{10-11} sts, work across in Pattern Stitch: 20{22-24} sts.

Row 2: Work across in Pattern Stitch.

Row 3: Bind off 10{11-12} sts, work across in Pattern Stitch: 10{11-12} sts.

Row 4: Work across in Pattern Stitch.

Bind off remaining sts.

SLEEVE (Make 2)
RIBBING
With smaller size needles, cast on 53{55-57} sts.

Row 1: P2, K1, (P1, K1) across to last 2 sts, P2.

Row 2 (Right side): K2, P1, (K1, P1) across to last 2 sts, K2.

Repeat Rows 1 and 2 until Ribbing measures approximately $\frac{1}{2}$" (12 mm), ending by working Row 2.

Decrease Row: Purl across decreasing 3 sts evenly spaced: 50{52-54} sts.

BODY
Change to larger size needles.

Row 1 (Right side): K2, purl across to last 2 sts, K2.

Row 2: P2, knit across to last 2 sts, P2.

Rows 3-6: Repeat Rows 1 and 2 twice.

Row 7 (Increase row): K2, M1P *(Figs. 5a & b, page 47)*, purl across to last 2 sts, M1P, K2: 52{54-56} sts.

Continuing in established pattern and maintaining 2 edge sts worked in Stockinette Stitch at each edge, continue to increase one stitch at **each** edge in same manner, every 6th row, 9{15-21} times **more**; then increase every 8th row, 8{4-0} times *(see Zeros, page 44)*: 86{92-98} sts.

Work even until Sleeve measures approximately 17$\frac{1}{2}${18-18}"/44.5{45.5-45.5} cm from cast on edge, ending by working a **wrong** side row.

SLEEVE CAP
Maintain established pattern throughout.

Rows 1 and 2: Bind off 8{10-12} sts, work across: 70{72-74} sts.

Rows 3 and 4: Bind off 2{3-3} sts, work across: 66{66-68} sts.

Row 5 (Decrease row): K1, SSK, purl across to last 3 sts, K2 tog, K1: 64{64-66} sts.

Row 6: P2, knit across to last 2 sts, P2.

Rows 7 thru 42{44-46}: Repeat Rows 5 and 6, 18{19-20} times: 28{26-26} sts.

Last 4 Rows: Bind off 2 sts, work across: 20{18-18} sts.

Bind off remaining sts.

FINISHING
Sew shoulder seams.

Sew Sleeves into armholes matching bound off sts at underarm and placing center of Cap at shoulder seam.

Weave underarm and side in one continuous seam (*Fig. 9, page 48*).

NECK RIBBING
With **right** side facing and using smaller size needles, pick up 155{155-157} sts evenly spaced around entire Neck edge (*Figs. 8a & b, page 48*).

Row 1: P2, K1, (P1, K1) across to last 2 sts, P2.

Row 2 (Right side): K2, P1, (K1, P1) across to last 2 sts, K2.

Row 3: P2, K1, (P1, K1) across to last 2 sts, P2.

Bind off all sts firmly in pattern.

LEFT BUTTON BAND
With **right** side facing and using smaller size needles, pick up 74{76-80} sts evenly spaced along Left Front edge.

Rows 1 and 2: Knit across.

Bind off all sts in **knit**.

RIGHT BUTTONHOLE BAND
With **right** side facing and using smaller size needles, pick up 74{76-80} sts evenly spaced along Right Front edge.

Row 1 (Buttonhole row): K3{4-3}, bind off next 2 sts, ★ K8{8-9}, bind off next 2 sts; repeat from ★ 5 times **more**, K2{3-2}: 60{62-66} sts.

Row 2: K3{4-3}, **turn**; add on 2 sts (*Figs. 7a & b, page 48*), **turn**; ★ K9{9-10}, **turn**; add on 2 sts, **turn**; repeat from ★ 5 times **more**, K3{4-3}: 74{76-80} sts.

Bind off all sts in **knit**.

Sew buttons to Left Front Band opposite buttonholes.

OPTION

DIVINE ASYMMETRY

1

Completely **unique** from fiber to finish, this upbeat cardigan opens on the diagonal. The llama/wool blend, medium-weight yarn retains plenty of **warmth**. You'll reach for this knit jacket time and again.

Easy-care yarn in a rich shade of green suggests a more **relaxed** mood. Snuggle into the **softness** of this sweater; then go out for a leisurely stroll. You'll never notice if the air is brisk outdoors, but everyone will notice how **fashionable** you look.

OPTION

Option 1

Classic Elite Yarns, Inc. Montera

Medium/Worsted Weight Yarn
  [$3^1/2$ ounces, 127 yards
  (100 grams, 116 meters) per skein]:
  7{9-11} skeins
Straight knitting needles, sizes 9 (5.5 mm) **and**
  10 (6 mm) **or** sizes needed for gauge
Yarn needle
Sewing needle and thread
$1^1/4$" (3 cm) Buttons - 6
Optional: $^1/2$" (12 mm) Buttons - 6 (to anchor
  larger buttons in place)

GAUGE: With larger size needles, in pattern,
  16 sts and 24 rows = 4" (10 cm)

DIVINE ASYMMETRY ▰▰▰▱ INTERMEDIATE

Option 2

TLC® Amoré™

MEDIUM 4

Medium/Worsted Weight Yarn
  [6 ounces, 290 yards
  (170 grams, 265 meters) per skein]:
  3{4-5} skeins
Straight knitting needles, sizes 9 (5.5 mm) **and**
  10 (6 mm) **or** sizes needed for gauge
Yarn needle
Sewing needle and thread
$1^1/4$" (3 cm) Buttons - 6
Optional: $^1/2$" (12 mm) Buttons - 6 (to anchor
  larger buttons in place)

GAUGE: With larger size needles, in pattern,
  16 sts and 24 rows = 4" (10 cm)

Size	Finished Chest Measurement
Small	39$\frac{1}{2}$" (100.5 cm)
Medium	46$\frac{1}{2}$" (118 cm)
Large	53$\frac{1}{2}$" (136 cm)

Size Note: Instructions are written for size Small with sizes Medium and Large in braces { }. Instructions will be easier to read if you circle all the numbers pertaining to your size. If only one number is given, it applies to all sizes.

BLOCK PATTERN
(Multiple of 14 plus 7 sts)
The Block pattern is made up of Stockinette Stitch and Reverse Stockinette Stitch blocks, working each block across 7 sts for 8 rows. The pattern is established on Row 1, then reversed on Row 9. Maintain pattern when decreasing and increasing sts.

Row 1 (Right side): P7, (K7, P7) across.
Row 2: K7, (P7, K7) across.
Rows 3-8: Repeat Rows 1 and 2, 3 times.
Row 9: K7, (P7, K7) across.
Row 10: P7, (K7, P7) across.
Rows 11-16: Repeat Rows 9 and 10, 3 times.
Repeat Rows 1-16 for pattern.

BACK
RIBBING
With smaller size needles, cast on 89{103-117} sts.

Row 1 (Right side): K2, P1, (K1, P1) across to last 2 sts, K2.

Row 2: P2, K1, (P1, K1) across to last 2 sts, P2.

Repeat Rows 1 and 2 until Ribbing measures approximately 1$\frac{1}{2}$" (4 cm), ending by working Row 1.

Last Row: P2, work in established ribbing across to last 2 sts decreasing 8 sts evenly spaced (*see Decreasing Evenly Across A Row, page 45*), P2: 81{95-109} sts.

BODY
Change to larger size needles.

Row 1: K2, work in Block Pattern across to last 2 sts, K2.

Row 2: P2, work in Block Pattern across to last 2 sts, P2.

Rows 3-8: Repeat Rows 1 and 2, 3 times.

Row 9 (Decrease row): K1, SSK (*Figs. 3a-c, page 46*), work in established pattern across to last 3 sts, K2 tog (*Fig. 1, page 46*), K1: 79{93-107} sts.

Continue to decrease in same manner, every 4th row, 5 times **more**: 69{83-97} sts.

Work even until Back measures approximately 9" (23 cm) from cast on edge, ending by working a **wrong** side row.

Increase Row: K2, M1 (*Figs. 4a & b, page 46*), work in established pattern across to last 2 sts, M1, K2: 71{85-99} sts.

Continue to increase in same manner, working new sts in pattern, alternately every 4th and 6th row, 5 times **more**: 81{95-109} sts.

Work even until Back measures approximately 15$\frac{1}{2}$" (39.5 cm) from cast on edge, ending by working a **wrong** side row.

ARMHOLE SHAPING
Maintain established pattern throughout.

Rows 1 and 2: Bind off 4{6-8} sts, work across: 73{83-93} sts.

Instructions continued on page 40.

Row 3 (Decrease row): K1, SSK, work across to last 3 sts, K2 tog, K1: 71{81-91} sts.

Row 4: P2, work across to last 2 sts, P2.

Repeat Rows 3 and 4, 5{6-7} times: 61{69-77} sts.

Work even until Armholes measure approximately 8¼{8¾-9¼}"/21{22-23.5} cm, ending by working a **wrong** side row.

NECK & SHOULDER SHAPING
Both sides of Neck are worked at the same time, using separate yarn for **each** side.

Row 1: Bind off 5{7-8} sts at Armhole edge, work across next 20{22-25} sts; with second yarn, bind off next 9 sts, work across.

Rows 2-4: Bind off 5{7-8} sts at Armhole edge, work across; with second yarn, bind off 5 sts at Neck edge, work across.

Row 5: Bind off all sts on first side; with second yarn, bind off 5 sts at Neck edge, work across.

Bind off remaining sts.

LEFT FRONT
RIBBING
With smaller size needles, cast on 59{66-73} sts.

Row 1 (Right side): K2, P1, (K1, P1) across to last 2 sts, K2.

Row 2: P2, K1, (P1, K1) across to last 2 sts, P2.

Repeat Rows 1 and 2 until Ribbing measures approximately 1½" (4 cm), ending by working Row 1.

Last Row: P2, work across in established ribbing to last 2 sts decreasing 6 sts evenly spaced, P2: 53{60-67} sts.

BODY
Change to larger size needles.

Maintain 2 edge sts worked in Stockinette Stitch at **each** edge.

Row 1: K9, P7, (K7, P7) across to last 9{2-9} sts, K9{2-9}.

Row 2: P9{2-9}, K7, (P7, K7) across to last 9 sts, P9.

Rows 3-8: Repeat Rows 1 and 2, 3 times.

Row 9 (Decrease row): K1, SSK, P6, (K7, P7) across to last 2{9-2} sts, K2{9-2}: 52{59-66} sts.

Maintaining established pattern, continue to decrease in same manner, every 4th row, 5 times **more**: 47{54-61} sts.

Work even until Left Front measures approximately 9" (23 cm) from cast on edge, ending by working a **wrong** side row.

Increase Row: K2, M1, work across in established pattern: 48{55-62} sts.

Continue to increase in same manner, working new sts in pattern, alternately every 4th and 6th row, 5 times **more**: 53{60-67} sts.

Work even until Left Front measures approximately 15½" (39.5 cm) from cast on edge, ending by working a **wrong** side row.

ARMHOLE SHAPING
Maintain established pattern throughout.

Row 1: Bind off 4{6-8} sts, work across: 49{54-59} sts.

Row 2: P2, work across to last 2 sts, P2.

Row 3 (Decrease row): K1, SSK, work across: 48{53-58} sts.

Repeat Rows 2 and 3, 5{6-7} times: 43{47-51} sts.

Work even until Armhole measures approximately 6¼{6¾-7¼}"/16{17-18.5} cm, ending by working a **right** side row.

NECK SHAPING
Row 1: Bind off 17 sts, work across: 26{30-34} sts.

Row 2: K2, work across to last 2 sts, K2.

Row 3: Bind off 2 sts, work across: 24{28-32} sts.

Rows 4-12: Repeat Rows 2 and 3, 4 times; then repeat Row 2 once **more**: 16{20-24} sts.

SHOULDER SHAPING
Row 1: Bind off 5{7-8} sts, work across: 11{13-16} sts.

Row 2: Work across.

Rows 3 and 4: Repeat Rows 1 and 2: 6{6-8} sts.

Bind off remaining sts.

RIGHT FRONT
RIBBING
The Right Front is different from the Left Front, as it begins with fewer sts and has a diagonal edge.

With smaller size needles, cast on 37{44-51} sts.

Row 1 (Right side)**:** K2, P1, (K1, P1) across to last 2 sts, K2.

Row 2: P2, K1, (P1, K1) across to last 2 sts, P2.

Repeat Rows 1 and 2 until Ribbing measures approximately 1¹/₂" (4 cm), ending by working Row 1.

Last Row: P2, work across in established ribbing to last 2 sts decreasing 5 sts evenly spaced, P2: 32{39-46} sts.

BODY
Change to larger size needles.

Row 1: K2{9-2}, P7, (K7, P7) across to last 9 sts, K9.

Row 2: P9, K7, (P7, K7) across to last 2{9-2} sts, P2{9-2}.

Rows 3 and 4: Repeat Rows 1 and 2.

Row 5 (Increase row)**:** K2, M1, work across in established pattern: 33{40-47} sts.

Rows 6-8: Work across in established pattern.

Row 9 (Increase/Decrease row)**:** K2, M1, P1{0-1} **(see Zeros, page 44)**, K7{1-7}, (P7, K7) across to last 9 sts, P6, K2 tog, K1.

Continue to increase at same edge in same manner, working new sts in pattern, alternately every 4ᵗʰ and 6ᵗʰ row, 17 times **more** AND AT THE SAME TIME decrease at side edge in same manner, every 4ᵗʰ row, 5 times **more** then work even until Right Front measures approximately 9" (23 cm) from cast on edge; then increase alternately every 4ᵗʰ and 6ᵗʰ row, 6 times: 51{58-65} sts.

Work even until Right Front measures approximately 15¹/₂" (39.5 cm) from cast on edge, ending by working a **right** side row.

ARMHOLE SHAPING
Maintain established pattern throughout.

Row 1: Bind off 4{6-8} sts, work across: 47{52-57} sts.

Row 2 (Decrease row)**:** Work across to last 3 sts, K2 tog, K1: 46{51-56} sts.

Row 3: P2, work across to last 2 sts, P2.

Repeat Rows 2 and 3, 5{6-7} times: 41{45-49} sts.

Work even until Armhole measures approximately 6¹/₄{6³/₄-7¹/₄}"/16{17-18.5} cm, ending by working a **wrong** side row.

Instructions continued on page 42.

NECK SHAPING
Row 1: Bind off 15 sts, work across: 26{30-34} sts.

Row 2: P2, work across to last 2 sts, P2.

Row 3: Bind off 2 sts, work across: 24{28-32} sts.

Rows 4-11: Repeat Rows 2 and 3, 4 times: 16{20-24} sts.

SHOULDER SHAPING
Row 1: Bind off 5{7-8} sts, work across: 11{13-16} sts.

Row 2: Work across.

Rows 3 and 4: Repeat Rows 1 and 2: 6{6-8} sts.

Bind off remaining sts.

SLEEVE (Make 2)
RIBBING
With smaller size needles, cast on 45 sts.

Row 1 (Right side): K2, P1, (K1, P1) across to last 2 sts, K2.

Row 2: P2, K1, (P1, K1) across to last 2 sts, P2.

Repeat Rows 1 and 2 until Ribbing measures approximately 1¹/₂" (4 cm), ending by working Row 1.

Last Row: P2, work across in established ribbing to last 2 sts decreasing 6 sts evenly spaced, P2: 39 sts.

BODY
Change to larger size needles.

Row 1: K2, work in Block Pattern across to last 2 sts, K2.

Row 2: P2, work in Block Pattern across to last 2 sts, P2.

Rows 3-10: Repeat Rows 1 and 2, 4 times.

Row 11 (Increase row): K2, M1, work across in established pattern to last 2 sts, M1, K2: 41 sts.

Continue to increase in same manner, working new sts in pattern, every 8ᵗʰ row, 8{1-0} times; then increase every 6ᵗʰ row, 0{11-5} times; then increase every 4ᵗʰ row, 0{0-11} times: 57{65-73} sts.

Work even until Sleeve measures approximately 17¹/₂{18-18}"/44.5{45.5-45.5} cm from cast on edge, ending by working a **wrong** side row.

SLEEVE CAP
Maintain established pattern throughout.

Rows 1 and 2: Bind off 4{6-8} sts, work across: 49{53-57} sts.

Row 3 (Decrease row): K1, SSK, work across to last 3 sts, K2 tog, K1: 47{51-55} sts.

Row 4: P2, work across to last 2 sts, P2.

Rows 5-26: Repeat Rows 3 and 4, 11{12-13} times: 25{27-29} sts.

Rows 27-30: Bind off 2 sts, work across: 17{19-21} sts.

Bind off remaining sts.

FINISHING
LEFT FRONT BAND
With **right** side facing and using smaller size needles, pick up 91 sts evenly spaced along Left Front edge *(Fig. 8a, page 48)*.

Row 1: P1, (K1, P1) across.

Row 2: K1, (P1, K1) across.

Rows 3 and 4: Repeat Rows 1 and 2.

Bind off all sts in pattern.

RIGHT FRONT BAND

With **right** side facing and using smaller size needles, pick up 93 sts evenly spaced along Right Front edge.

Row 1: P1, (K1, P1) across.

Row 2: K1, (P1, K1) across.

Row 3 (Buttonhole row): P1, K1, bind off next 4 sts (buttonhole), ★ (K1, P1) 6 times, bind off next 4 sts (buttonhole); repeat from ★ 4 times **more**, P1: 69 sts.

Row 4: K1, P1, **turn**; add on 4 sts (*Figs. 7a & b, page 48*), **turn**; ★ (K1, P1) 6 times, K1, **turn**; add on 4 sts, **turn**; repeat from ★ 4 times **more**, P1, K1: 93 sts.

Rows 5-8: Repeat Rows 1 and 2 twice.

Bind off all sts in pattern.

COLLAR

With larger size needles, cast on 114 sts.

Row 1: P2, (K2, P2) across.

Row 2 (Right side): K2, (P2, K2) across.

Rows 3-5: Repeat Rows 1 and 2 once, then repeat Row 1 once **more**.

Row 6 (Decrease row): K1, SSK, work across in established ribbing to last 3 sts, K2 tog, K1: 112 sts.

Continue to decrease in same manner, every 4th row, 3 times **more**: 106 sts.

SHAPING
Row 1: P2, (K2, P2) across.

Row 2: Bind off 22 sts, work across: 84 sts.

Rows 3-14: Bind off 5 sts, work across: 24 sts.

Bind of remaining sts.

Pin **wrong** side of Collar to **right** side of Neck edge, matching the first long bound off edge of Collar to bound off edge of Right Front, and center of Collar to center of Back neck, and ending at center of Left Front; sew in place.

Sew Sleeves into armholes matching bound off sts at underarm and placing center of Cap at shoulder seam.

Weave Sleeve and side in one continuous seam (*Fig. 9, page 48*).

Lap Right Front over Left Front.
Sew buttons to Left Front opposite buttonholes. If you are using a heavy button, use a smaller button on the wrong side to anchor the weight of the larger button.

G E N E R A L

ABBREVIATIONS

ch(s)	chain(s)	Rnd(s)	Round(s)
cm	centimeters	SSK	slip, slip, knit
K	knit	st(s)	stitch(es)
M1	Make One	tbl	through back loop(s)
M1P	Make One Purl	tog	together
mm	millimeters	YO	yarn over(s)
P	purl		

★ — work instructions following ★ as many **more** times as indicated in addition to the first time.

( ) or [ ] — work enclosed instructions **as many** times as specified by the number immediately following **or** contains explanatory remarks.

colon (:) — the number(s) given after a colon at the end of a row or round denote(s) the number of stitches you should have on that row or round.

work even — work without increasing or decreasing in the established pattern.

GAUGE

Exact gauge is essential for proper fit. Needle sizes given in instructions are merely guides and should never be used without first making a sample swatch approximately 4" (10 cm) square in the stitch, yarn, and needles specified. Then measure it, counting your stitches and rows carefully. If you have more stitches per inch than specified, try again with larger size needles; if fewer, try again with a smaller size. If you have more rows per inch than specified, use a larger size needle for the purl rows; if fewer, use a smaller size needle for the purl rows. Keep trying until you find the size that will give you the specified gauge. DO NOT HESITATE TO CHANGE NEEDLE SIZE TO OBTAIN CORRECT GAUGE. Once proper gauge is obtained, measure width of garment approximately every 3" (7.5 cm) to be sure gauge remains consistent.

MARKERS

As a convenience to you, we have used markers to help distinguish the beginning of a pattern or round. Place markers as instructed. You may use purchased markers or tie a length of contrasting color yarn around the needle. When you reach a marker on each row or round, slip it from the left needle to the right needle; remove it when no longer needed.

ZEROS

To consolidate the length of an involved pattern, Zeros are sometimes used so that all sizes can be combined. For example, increase one stitch at each edge, every 6th row, 0{3-7} times means the first size would do nothing, the second size would increase 3 times, and the largest size would increase 7 times.

INSTRUCTIONS

KNITTING NEEDLES		
UNITED STATES	ENGLISH U.K.	METRIC (mm)
0	13	2
1	12	2.25
2	11	2.75
3	10	3.25
4	9	3.5
5	8	3.75
6	7	4
7	6	4.5
8	5	5
9	4	5.5
10	3	6
10½	2	6.5
11	1	8
13	00	9
15	000	10
17	---	12.75
19	---	15

KNIT TERMINOLOGY	
UNITED STATES	INTERNATIONAL
gauge =	tension
bind off =	cast off
yarn over (YO) =	yarn forward (yfwd) **or** yarn around needle (yrn)

Yarn Weight Symbol & Names	SUPER FINE 1	FINE 2	LIGHT 3	MEDIUM 4	BULKY 5	SUPER BULKY 6
Type of Yarns in Category	Sock, Fingering Baby	Sport, Baby	DK, Light Worsted	Worsted, Afghan, Aran	Chunky, Craft, Rug	Bulky, Roving
Knit Gauge Ranges in Stockinette St to 4" (10 cm)	27-32 sts	23-26 sts	21-24 sts	16-20 sts	12-15 sts	6-11 sts
Advised Needle Size Range	1-3	3-5	5-7	7-9	9-11	11 and larger

■□□□ BEGINNER	Projects for first-time knitters using basic knit and purl stitches. Minimal shaping.	
■■□□ EASY	Projects using basic stitches, repetitive stitch patterns, simple color changes, and simple shaping and finishing.	
■■■□ INTERMEDIATE	Projects with a variety of stitches, such as basic cables and lace, simple intarsia, double-pointed needles and knitting in the round needle techniques, mid-level shaping and finishing.	
■■■■ EXPERIENCED	Projects using advanced techniques and stitches, such as short rows, fair isle, more intricate intarsia, cables, lace patterns, and numerous color changes.	

DECREASING EVENLY ACROSS A ROW

Add one to the number of decreases required and divide that number into the number of stitches on the needle(s). Subtract one from the result and the new number is the approximate number of stitches to be worked between each decrease. Adjust the number as needed.

THROUGH BACK LOOP
(abbreviated tbl)

When instructed to work through back loop of a stitch, insert right needle as indicated *(Figs. A & B)*.

Fig. A

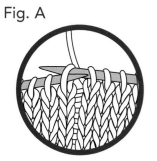

Fig. B

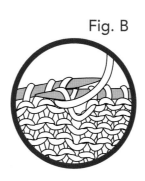

KNIT 2 TOGETHER
(abbreviated K2 tog)
Insert the right needle into the **front** of the first two stitches on the left needle as if to **knit** (*Fig. 1*), then **knit** them together as if they were one stitch.

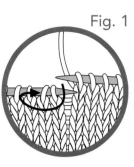
Fig. 1

PURL 2 TOGETHER
(abbreviated P2 tog)
Insert the right needle into the **front** of the first two stitches on the left needle as if to **purl** (*Fig. 2*), then purl them together.

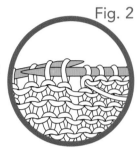
Fig. 2

SLIP, SLIP, KNIT *(abbreviated SSK)*
With yarn in back of work, separately slip two stitches as if to **knit** (*Fig. 3a*). Insert the **left** needle into the **front** of both slipped stitches (*Fig. 3b*) and knit them together (*Fig. 3c*).

Fig. 3a

Fig. 3b

Fig. 3c

MAKE ONE *(abbreviated M1)*
Insert the left needle under the horizontal strand between the stitches from the **front** (*Fig. 4a*). Then knit into the **back** of the strand (*Fig. 4b*).

Fig. 4a

Fig. 4b

MAKE ONE PURLWISE (abbreviated M1P)

Insert the **left** needle under the horizontal strand between the stitches from the **back** *(Fig. 5a)*. Then purl the strand *(Fig. 5b)*.

Fig. 5a

Fig. 5b

YARN OVERS

After a knit stitch, before a knit stitch
Bring the yarn forward **between** the needles, then back **over** the top of the right hand needle, so that it is now in position to knit the next stitch *(Fig. 6a)*.

Fig. 6a

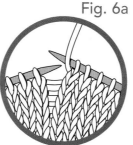

After a purl stitch, before a purl stitch
Take yarn **over** the right hand needle to the back, then forward **under** it, so that it is now in position to purl the next stitch *(Fig. 6b)*.

Fig. 6b

After a knit stitch, before a purl stitch
Bring yarn forward **between** the needles, then back **over** the top of the right hand needle and forward **between** the needles again, so that it is now in position to purl the next stitch *(Fig. 6c)*.

Fig. 6c

After a purl stitch, before a knit stitch
Take yarn **over** right hand needle to the back, so that it is now in position to knit the next stitch *(Fig. 6d)*.

Fig. 6d

ADDING NEW STITCHES

Insert the right needle into stitch as if to **knit**, yarn over and pull loop through *(Fig. 7a)*, insert the left needle into the loop just worked from **front** to **back** and slip the loop onto the left needle *(Fig. 7b)*. Repeat for required number of stitches.

Fig. 7a

Fig. 7b

PICKING UP STITCHES

When instructed to pick up stitches, insert the needle from the **front** to the **back** under two strands at the edge of the worked piece *(Figs. 8a & b)*. Put the yarn around the needle as if to **knit**, then bring the needle with the yarn back through the stitch to the right side, resulting in a stitch on the needle.
Repeat this along the edge, picking up the required number of stitches.
A crochet hook may be helpful to pull yarn through.

Fig. 8a

Fig. 8b

WEAVING SEAMS

Fig. 9

With the **right** side of both pieces facing you and edges even, sew through both sides once to secure the seam. Insert the needle under the bar **between** the first and second stitches on the row and pull the yarn through *(Fig. 9)*. Insert the needle under the next bar on the second side. Repeat from side to side, being careful to match rows. If the edges are different lengths, it may be necessary to insert the needle under two bars at one edge.